Tested for Safety

Contents

Dina McClellan

Safer Bikes

Today, many people ride bicycles.
The bikes they ride have special parts
to make riding safer and more fun.
Long ago, bike riding was not very safe.

These high wheelers were hard to ride. They were easy to tip over and there were no brakes!

Then a man named J. K. Starley made a new kind of bike. Safety bicycles solved many of the problems people had with high wheelers.

These bikes were a big hit.

Starley's Safety Bicycle

Rubber tires filled with air made the ride a lot less bumpy.

Brakes let the bike coast to a stop.

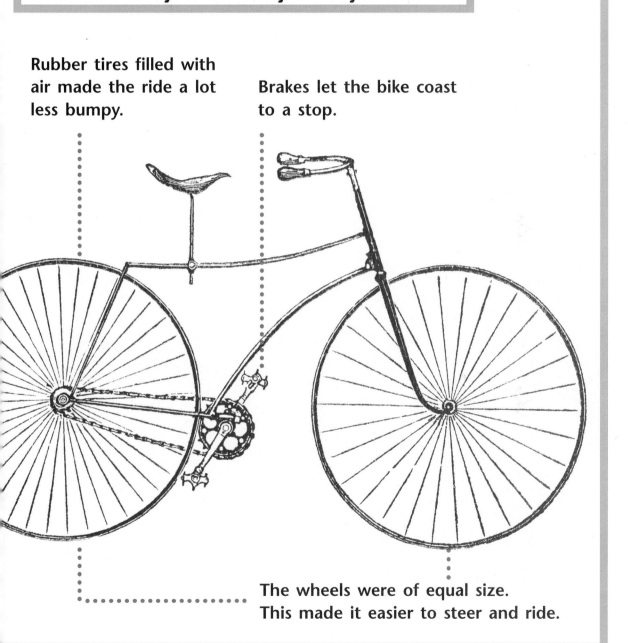

The wheels were of equal size. This made it easier to steer and ride.

Over the years bikes have become safer and safer.
The brakes we have now work much better.
Reflectors keep riders safe at night.

Bike helmets protect riders
from getting hurt.

Today, you can see many cars traveling on all kinds of roads.

This old cartoon shows the problems early drivers had.

Long ago, the first cars traveled on roads that had been made for horses and wagons. Drivers had no rules to help them know when to go or stop.

Inventor Garrett Morgan

Inventors worked on ways to make driving safer. An inventor named Garrett Morgan made a traffic signal. Now drivers knew when to stop and when to go.

Today, we still use traffic signals that are based on Mr. Morgan's ideas.

Cars also have new parts to help make driving safer. Air bags, seat belts, and anti-lock brakes are all checked before a car leaves the factory. Dummies are used in safety tests. If the car passes a test, real people will be safe, too.

Special clothing can help keep people safe.

Firefighters need to protect themselves from smoke and flames. The shiny material in these suits helps keep the firefighters safe because it will not burn.

Other workers also use special safety equipment. These workers wear hard hats and safety straps.

This scientist wears goggles to protect her eyes when she works with a laser.

This amazing suit makes it safe for the astronaut to take a walk in space.
New safety equipment allows people to do things that they could not have done before.